FEMALE FIRSTS IN THEIR FIELDS

Air & Space

Broadcasting & Journalism

Business & Industry

Entertainment & Performing Arts

Government & Politics

Literature

Science & Medicine

Sports & Athletics

FEMALE FIRSTS IN THEIR FIELDS

BROADCASTING
&
JOURNALISM

Anne E. Hill

Introduction by
Roslyn Rosen

CHELSEA HOUSE PUBLISHERS
Philadelphia

For the women who inspire me:
Mom, Tia, Aunt Julie, Aunt Annie, and Ella

Produced by P. M. Gordon Associates, Inc.
Philadelphia, Pennsylvania

Editor in Chief Stephen Reginald
Managing Editor James D. Gallagher
Production Manager Pamela Loos
Art Director Sara Davis
Director of Photography Judy L. Hasday
Senior Production Editor Lisa Chippendale
Publishing Coordinator James McAvoy

Picture research by Gillian Speeth, Picture This
Cover illustration by Cliff Spohn
Cover design by Keith Trego

Frontispiece: Barbara Walters and Diane Sawyer

The Chelsea House World Wide Web site address is
http://www.chelseahouse.com

3 5 7 9 8 6 4 2

Library of Congress Cataloging-in-Publication Data

Hill, Anne E.
      Female firsts in their fields. Broadcasting & journalism /
    Anne E. Hill.
        p. cm.
      Includes bibliographical references and index.
      Summary: Examines the lives and careers of Barbara Walters, Diane
    Sawyer, Ida Tarbell, Ellen Goodman, Helen Thomas, and Hannah Storm.
      ISBN 0-7910-5139-0 (hardcover)
      1. Women journalists–United States–Biography–Juvenile literature.
    2. Women broadcasters–United States–Biography–Juvenile literature.
    [1. Journalists. 2. Broadcasters. 3. Women–Biography.] I. Title.
    PN4820.H55 1998
    070′.92′273–dc21
      [B]   98-44005
                                                                CIP
                                                                 AC

CONTENTS

INTRODUCTION

Roslyn Rosen

W hen I was a toddler, it struck me that the other people in my family's New York apartment building were different. They did not use their hands when they talked, and they did not have to watch each other speak. I had been born deaf, and I felt sorry for them because they did not know the joy of drawing pictures in the air. They could not splash ideas into the air with a jab of the finger or a wave of the hand. Not until later did I realize the downside of being deaf—I couldn't communicate directly with my grandparents and extended family members, I depended on others to make important phone calls for me, and I found life's opportunities narrower, in part because I had few deaf (let alone female) role models.

Gallaudet University in Washington, D.C., is the only college for deaf students in the world. I arrived there in September 1958. It was a haven where sign language was part of the educational process, where there were deaf professors, and where opportunities for extracurricular leadership abounded. At Gallaudet I met deaf female professionals for the first time, although there were probably not more than three or four. The president and administrators of Gallaudet were all males who could hear—typical of school administrations during those years.

In my first month at Gallaudet, I also met the man who would become my husband. My destiny was charted: major in something that I could use as a homemaker (since that would be my job), get married, have a bunch of kids, and live happily ever after. This was the expectation for women in the late 1950s and early 1960s. And I stuck to the script: I majored in art with an emphasis on education and English, got married, and had three children. My life was complete–or so I thought.

The 1960s were turbulent and thought-provoking years. The civil rights movement and the beginnings of a women's movement emphasized human rights and equality for all. I came to see how alike the issues were that faced women, people of color, and people with disabilities, in terms of human rights and respect for human differences. Multicultural studies are vital for this understanding. Changes were occurring at an accelerating rate. Those changes affected my husband and me by broadening our traditional gender roles. With my husband's support, I pursued a master's degree in education of deaf students and later a doctoral degree in education administration. From my first job as a part-time sign language teacher, I eventually joined the faculty at Gallaudet University. In 1981 I was promoted to dean of the College for Continuing Education, and in 1993, to vice president for academic affairs.

During the formative years of my career, many of my role models and mentors were deaf men who had reached positions of leadership. They hired, taught, advised, and encouraged me. There were times when I felt the effects of the "glass ceiling" (an invisible barrier that keeps women or minorities from rising any higher). Sometimes I needed to depend on my male colleagues because my access to "old boy" networks or decision makers was limited. When I became involved with the National Association of the Deaf (NAD), the world's oldest organization of deaf people, I met deaf women who became role models–Dr. Gertie Galloway was the first deaf female president of the NAD, and Marcella Meyer had founded the Greater Los Angeles Community Service of the Deaf (GLAD). In 1980 I was elected to the board of directors of the National Association of the Deaf, and in 1990, I became the second woman elected president of NAD.

When I became a dean at Gallaudet in 1981, I also became a member of the school's Council of Deans, which at the time included only two deaf deans and two female deans. I was the only deaf woman dean. The vice president was a white male, and he once commented that top administrators often build management teams in their own image. I have found that to be true. As a dean, I was the highest-ranking deaf woman at Gallaudet, and I was able to hire and help a number of young deaf female professionals within the College for Continuing Education and our regional centers around the country. In the five years that I have been vice president at Gallaudet I have added many deaf, female, and minority members to my own management team. When I was the president of NAD, I hired its first deaf female executive director, Nancy Bloch. I also encouraged two of my friends, Mabs Holcomb and Sharon Wood, to write the first deaf women history book, a source of inspiration for young deaf girls.

It is important for women who have reached the top levels of their fields to advise and help younger women to become successful. It is also important for young girls to know about the groundbreaking contributions of women who came before them. The women profiled in this series of biographies overcame many obstacles to succeed. Some had physical handicaps, others fought generations of discriminatory attitudes toward women in the workplace. The world may never provide equal opportunities for every human being, but we can all work together to improve life for the next generation.

DR. ROSLYN ROSEN is the Vice President for Academic Affairs at Gallaudet University in Washington, D.C. Dr. Rosen has served as a board member and President of the National Association of the Deaf (NAD), the oldest consumer organization in the world, and was a member of the National Captioning Institute's executive board for nine years. She is currently a board member of the World Federation of the Deaf. Dr. Rosen also wears the hats of daughter, wife, mother, and proud grandmother.

IDA TARBELL

Today, we're not surprised to see a woman reporting the news on television. We're used to reading a woman's name at the top of a newspaper column. But at one time people would have found either of these strange, and even shocking.

Since television has only been a popular medium since the mid-20th century, the history of women in broadcasting is short. But the history of American women in journalism dates back to colonial times–to 1731, when Elizabeth Timothy and her husband went into business with Benjamin Franklin. Elizabeth Timothy became a journalist after her husband died of smallpox and she took over the business.

Other women journalists followed her in that pioneering century, including Anna Zenger, Ann Franklin, and Mary Katherine Goddard. All were criticized for their bold and aggressive behavior–choosing a career instead of marriage. These pioneers were forced to choose between career and marriage because society would not allow them to have both.

One of these career women was Ida Minerva Tarbell. She

A clear-eyed Ida Tarbell in middle age, after she had made her reputation as the "Lady Muckraker."

believed that some women have "bachelor souls" and should not marry, but forge a career path for similar women to follow. Born in Erie County, Pennsylvania, on November 5, 1857, Ida was raised to believe in women's liberation, the freedom of women to have the same rights as men.

Her mother, Esther McCullough, was a feminist who taught school for six years before she married Franklin Tarbell. She resented having to sacrifice her teaching career for a family. Naming her daughter Ida Minerva was Esther's secret way of rebelling against that tradition. "Ida" was a character in Alfred Lord Tennyson's *The Princess,* who promoted higher education for women, while "Minerva" was the Greek goddess of wisdom.

Ida Tarbell grew up in the oil boom town of Rouseville, Pennsylvania, with her brother, William, and her sister, Sarah. Her younger brother, Franklin Jr., died of scarlet fever at age three. From a young age, Ida was aware that her mother was unhappy about marrying instead of continuing her career. When her mother entertained women's suffrage leaders—people who were working to get women the right to vote—Ida heard them talk about women's equality. She grew up wanting to attend college and have a career. Both of these notions were unheard of for women of her day. However, Esther supported her daughter's desire to go to college, against her father's wishes.

But when Ida graduated from high school in 1876, her father allowed her to attend Allegheny College, a coeducational college in the nearby town of Meadville, Pennsylvania. She was the only woman in her class, and only ten women had graduated from Allegheny since the school had first admitted women in 1870.

Away at college, Ida could explore her interests

Tarbell in 1904, the year her groundbreaking exposé of Standard Oil was published in two volumes.

among people who thought of her as a student first, not a woman. That freedom led Ida to believe that she would work as a biologist when she graduated. But no one would hire a woman biologist in 1880.

Instead of becoming a biologist, Ida became a teacher, like most females who wanted a career. But she found teaching unfulfilling, and she took a job annotating, writing, and editing articles for the Chautauqua Assembly's Methodist newspaper, the *Daily Herald*, and its magazine, *The Chautauquan,* in Meadville. Here Ida discovered her talent for writing.

As part of her job, she wrote profiles of prominent women in history—Madame de Stael, Marie Antoinette, and Madame Roland, an 18th-century woman who was a mother, wife, and leading revolutionary figure. Madame Roland became Ida's heroine. Unable to break free of what society thought she should do—marry and have children—Ida saw Roland as the woman who was able to have it all. She dreamed of one day traveling to France to write Roland's biography.

In 1890, she made that dream come true. A disagreement with her boss forced Ida to leave her position at the newspaper and magazine, and she went to France, supporting herself by freelance writing for magazines. People warned Ida that it was a mistake to leave Pennsylvania for a foreign country where she did not know the language and had no friends. Her minister told her that she was not a writer.

"But if I was not a writer," Ida believed, "I had certain qualifications for the practice of the modest kind of journalism on which I had decided. . . . Then there was my habit of steady, painstaking work—that ought to count for something. And perhaps I could learn to write." In time, 33-year-old Ida Tarbell would prove herself a more than competent writer.

Once she began to research Madame Roland, Ida grew disillusioned with her subject. Love and personal ambition, Ida believed, had made Madame Roland weak. This seemed to provide even more evidence for the popular belief that women must choose between love and career. But Ida was not one to give up on a project once she had begun, and she continued Madame Roland's biography.

In 1892, Tarbell was approached by the man who would help make hers a household name—Samuel Sidney McClure. McClure was a writer who wanted to start his own magazine. He would name it *McClure's,* and it would focus on reforming the injustices of the world. Sam McClure intended to gath-

A literary reunion in 1925: Sam McClure, standing, chats with his famous former employees Willa Cather (left) and Ida Tarbell, who served as editors at McClure's *in the early years of the century. With them is another noted journalist, Will Irwin.*

er only the best writers for his staff, so Ida was flattered by his offer and tempted by the idea of working in the cosmopolitan city of Manhattan, where the magazine would be based. She decided to write freelance articles for *McClure's* and send them to New York City until she finished her book. She would then return to the States to work with Sam McClure full time. Her book *Madame Roland: A Biography* was published by Scribners in 1896.

Meanwhile, in 1894, Ida arrived in Manhattan and her biographical sketches began appearing in each issue of *McClure's*. Among her first subjects were Napoleon Bonaparte and Abraham Lincoln. The popular series of illustrated biographies, which ran in installments, increased *McClure's* circulation and made Ida Tarbell famous. These articles were later published as books: *The Life of Abraham Lincoln* in 1900, and *A Life of Napoleon Bonaparte* in 1901.

Ida spent a lot of time researching these maga-

Tarbell works at her desk in 1921. In her later years she regretted having to give up a personal life to pursue her career, though she had paved the way for today's women to have greater opportunities.

zine biographies, but it was her investigative reporting that would cement her place in journalism, until then a man's world. From 1902 to 1904, *McClure's* ran Ida's articles on the history of Standard Oil. They were then gathered and published as two books in 1904. In her articles, she convinced the public that John D. Rockefeller, the owner of Standard Oil, was forcing smaller, independent oil companies out of business.

Ida's search for the truth about Standard Oil may have stemmed from loyalty to her father, who worked in the oil industry, and from her hometown's dependence on the oil business. Whatever her motive, Tarbell's exposé of the Standard Oil Trust Company prompted the federal government to investigate and brought down the massive Rockefeller family trust in 1911. Unfortunately, Ida's father did not live to see his daughter's success. Franklin died in 1905 and never knew the profound effect Ida had on the oil business.

Ida was not the only talented investigative journalist at *McClure's*. The magazine's other writers were also exposing injustices, from political corruption to the poor conditions mine workers faced. While the public found the articles absorbing and enlightening, the government wanted the attacks on the government and on government-controlled businesses to stop.

Outraged at the *McClure's* writers, President Theodore Roosevelt labeled them "muckrakers." He got the idea for the term from a character in John Bunyan's book, *The Pilgrim's Progress.* In that book, the man with the muckrake concentrated so hard on raking the filth (the muck) around his feet, he never noticed the pureness of the vast heavens above him. But Ida was not a man with a muckrake; she was a woman. She soon became known as the "Lady Muckraker."

The work of Ida and her co-workers fueled the Progressive Movement, a movement formed to fight the dominance of large corporations. By the early 1900s, the United States was full of businesses and trusts that controlled entire industries. Many of them did not care about the interests or conditions of working people. Another "muckraker" like Tarbell was Upton Sinclair, whose book *The Jungle* exposed the unsanitary conditions of the meat-packing industry. These writers brought the injustices of big corporations to the attention of the American public.

But in 1906, despite her new-found fame, Ida left

Tarbell in her eighties, identified in a newspaper caption as "dean of American women writers."

McClure's magazine. Although she considered Sam McClure her mentor and friend, they disagreed on the direction of the magazine. McClure wanted to create businesses that focused on solving the problems the magazine uncovered. He wanted to build a university, a library, a bank, an insurance company, and a low-cost housing project.

Tarbell thought these ideas conflicted with the belief upon which the magazine was founded—that big businesses were basically corrupt. Her departure from *McClure's* was another turning point in her career.

Ida and several fellow writers started the *American Magazine*, and she continued to write. Although she was far more forward thinking than most people of her day, Ida was disappointed in some of her own decisions. While women today can have marriage and children as well as a successful career, Ida had to give up a personal life to have a professional one. Later in life, she regretted not having both.

Her articles for the *American Magazine*, later published as the books *The Business of Being a Woman* and *The Ways of Woman*, expressed her beliefs that a woman's most important roles were as wife and mother. She proclaimed herself an antisuffragist, meaning she was against women's right to vote.

Many people were surprised at Ida's change of heart. Her writings seemed to contradict her career and life's work. In *The Business of Being a Woman*, she reveals her own difficult experiences as she made her mark in a man's world: For a woman to succeed, she wrote, "she must suppress her natural emotions and meet the world with a surface as non-resilient as she conceives that of man to be in his dealings with the world. . . . She must overcome her own bonds, . . . if she is to do her work."

Ida Tarbell paid her price for being a female pioneer. While her writing inspired future generations of women, when she died in 1944 she still believed that she could have made a greater contribution by staying home and having children. But it was the work of Ida Tarbell, and the work of dedicated women like her, that made it possible for women like those in the rest of this book to have both professional and personal lives.

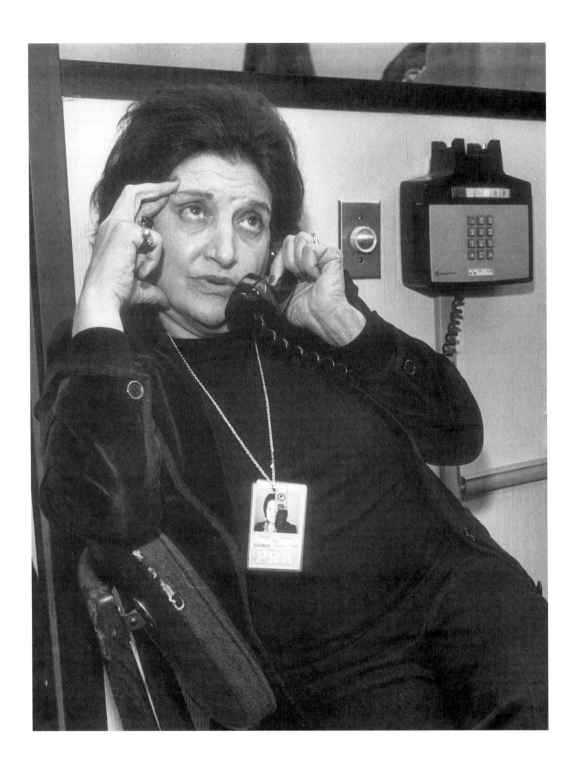

HELEN THOMAS

"**W**omen reporters have had to break down doors of press strongholds," Helen Thomas once said. "But once the doors have been opened, I have made it a policy to walk right in." By walking through doors and breaking down barriers, Helen Thomas has helped ensure that today's female journalists and their reporting get the respect they deserve.

Born in Winchester, Kentucky, on August 4, 1920, Helen was the seventh of George and Mary Thomas's nine children. Her parents had emigrated from Lebanon in 1903 and settled in Kentucky with other relatives already living there. Times were hard financially, and the family struggled. Neither parent could read or write, so George Thomas peddled a variety of goods until he saved enough money to open a grocery store. When the family moved to Detroit, Michigan, in 1924, he opened another neighborhood grocery store.

Although they may have lacked some material possessions, Helen, her six sisters, and two brothers lived surrounded by the love and kindness of their parents in a neighborhood rich in its variety of people and traditions. In 1929, after the stock market crashed and the Great Depression settled in,

Helen Thomas at work as White House bureau chief for UPI.

many of their neighbors lost their jobs. George Thomas donated food to those who needed it.

The Thomases instilled compassion, a sense of self-worth, and a deep commitment to learning in each of their children. They taught their children both Arab and American traditions; all of them grew up believing that they could "be somebody," Helen recalled. The girls and boys were treated equally in the Thomas family, and perhaps the lively dinner-table conversations about history and literature inspired them—eventually all nine children attended college.

By the time she entered Eastern High School in Detroit, Helen was already inquisitive, and when she worked on the school paper, she found the perfect outlet for her endless questions. "A teacher praised my work—and I liked the bylines!" Helen wrote in her book *Dateline: White House.* She decided she wanted to be a journalist.

In 1938, after graduating from high school, while many of her friends were getting married and starting families, Helen enrolled at Detroit's city college, which is now Wayne State University. To pay for her education, Thomas worked in the library and in the gas station owned by one of her brothers. She spent her free time writing for the campus newspaper. Four years later she graduated with a bachelor of arts degree in English.

The United States was in the middle of World War II when Thomas moved to Washington, D.C., in 1942. Eager for a job at a big-city paper, Helen worked as a restaurant hostess until she got her break as a copy girl at the *Washington Daily News.* Her starting salary was $17 a week. Although her main responsibilities were getting coffee and dough-nuts for the reporters and editors, Thomas considered herself lucky to have the job.

Her favorite moments came when she was allowed to hover near the news ticker, listening to the bells that signaled the break of a new story. She loved the excitement of the job. When her mother asked Helen when she was coming home, Helen realized that Washington, D.C., was where she would stay.

Her determination to be a journalist paid off when she was promoted to reporter at the paper. She didn't have time to report many stories, for she lost her job not long after when the *Daily News* had to cut back on staff for economic reasons. Thomas found a job at a news service, United Press, now called UPI–United Press International. With her new position came a raise to $24 a week and new responsibilities. She wrote local radio news, reporting to work at 5:30 A.M. Even though she knew she had been hired primarily because most of the qualified young men reporters were being drafted into the army, Thomas took advantage of the opportunity. In the next few years she more than proved herself the equal of a male reporter, and she kept her job even after thousands of male veterans returned to the work force in 1945.

In the late 1940s and early 1950s, Thomas wrote her own column, "Names in the News," which covered the activities of Washington celebrities. And in 1955 she was given an even greater responsibility: a regular "beat," an area assigned specifically to one reporter. She began by covering the U.S. Department of Justice, and her beat grew to include the

As president of the Women's National Press Club, Thomas (left) pins a corsage on First Lady Mamie Eisenhower, who visited in 1959 to celebrate her 63rd birthday and the club's 40th.

Thomas interviews John F. Kennedy at Georgetown Hospital after the birth of his son, John F. Kennedy Jr.

FBI, the Department of Health, Education, and Welfare, and the area for which she is most well-known—Capitol Hill, the White House, and the presidency.

In November 1960, at age 40, Thomas was assigned to cover newly elected president John F. Kennedy's Palm Beach, Florida, vacation. Here, her true reporting ability shone through. While UPI expected her to report on the "soft" stories involving the president's family, Thomas stepped up and appeared among the many male faces at presidential press conferences and daily briefings, asking the tough questions and demanding answers. In her first White House assignment in January 1961, Thomas began closing the press conferences with the now traditional phrase, "Thank you, Mr. President."

The year before, Thomas had been elected president of the Women's National Press Club. The club was founded in 1919 to rally female reporters into a group similar to the National Press Club, which was open exclusively to male reporters. At National Press Club luncheons, top government officials and visiting foreign dignitaries often gave major speeches. Although female reporters had been permitted to cover luncheon speeches at the club since 1955, they had to sit in the balcony away from the action on the floor, too far away to fire off questions at the visiting speakers, and out of reach of the phones that they needed to call in their stories.

Helen Thomas led the crusade for women to be allowed equal access to the National Press Club. She won a small victory when Soviet premier Nikita Khrushchev insisted that women be allowed on the floor at his Press Club speech. President Kennedy was on the side of the women as well—he threatened not to speak at the club unless female reporters were allowed on the floor. Encouraged, women reporters continued their campaign, with Thomas at the helm. Finally, in 1971, after a decade-long battle, the National Press Club admitted women, and Thomas became its first female officer.

There was another new role in store for Thomas—wife. On October 16, 1971, after decades of believing that she, like Ida Tarbell, had to choose between career and marriage, Thomas married Associated Press reporter Douglas Cornell. Her marriage was happy and her career successful. (Cornell died in 1982.)

Thomas continued to work. She was the only female print journalist to accompany President Nixon on his trip to China in 1972. Perhaps she

Thomas welcomes Vice President Al Gore, his wife Tipper Gore, and President Bill Clinton to the Gridiron Club in 1993. Thomas was the club's first female member–and then its first female president.

owes her rise in the ranks of reporting to her unique ability to confront world leaders. "[I] treat them like other human beings," Thomas said. "I don't bow and I don't scrape. I don't ask for their autographs. I cover them. They deserve respect, but not awe and certainly not fear."

But Thomas *was* in awe when, in 1974, she was named UPI bureau chief at the White House. After more than 30 years in the field, she had reached the top of her profession. "I have seen presidents in moments of glory bursting with their own sense of being, caught up in public adulation," Thomas later said of her profession. "I have also seen presidents in despair, overburdened, brooding, emotional, seeking understanding." Thomas admits that she "will never be blasé about covering the White House." For the last half century, Thomas has known and followed the professional and personal lives of every U.S. president, including John Kennedy, Lyndon Johnson, Richard Nixon, Gerald Ford, Jimmy Carter, Ronald Reagan, George Bush, and Bill Clinton.

Besides her extremely busy work schedule, Helen Thomas continues to hold offices in clubs. In 1975, she became the first female president of the White House Correspondents' Association and the first female member of the Gridiron Club. She published her book *Dateline: White House*, an account of her personal look at America's presidents and their families, the same year. She has been awarded 24 honorary degrees, and she frequently lectures and gives commencement addresses at colleges and universities.

While her direct and often hard-hitting journalistic style has drawn criticism, Thomas continues to report the White House goings-on as she sees them. "I love covering my beat. It's a thrill and will remain one for so long as I can feel the great contribution a reporter can make is to keep an eye on the presidency. For in doing so, she is helping to keep an eye on democracy—to keep it alive." When asked whether she will retire soon, Thomas replied, "I would like to die with my boots on—with pen and notebook in hand."

Helen Thomas sees the strides that women in her field have made in recent years, but she claims that "we have more mountains to climb and we shouldn't rest until we get there." She does admit her secret joy that male reporters now, "like everyone else, get their own coffee and doughnuts."

BARBARA WALTERS

Barbara Walters was not the first female television journalist, but she was the first to have such significant success, and her face has since become the most recognizable on television. Walters is also one of the most well paid. The $1 million salary awarded to her in 1976 was the most ever paid to a broadcaster—male or female.

Born on September 25, 1929, Barbara Jill Walters had two loving parents, Lou and Dena. Their firstborn child, a son named Burton, had died of pneumonia when he was only one year old. Barbara's older sister, Jacqueline, was mentally handicapped and needed most of her parents' energy and attention. Barbara often felt isolated from her own family.

When Barbara was growing up her family's financial situation was constantly changing. Her father, Lou, had a passion for gambling and often went too far on his bets. He ran a talent agency and when luck was on his side, he opened a nightclub in Boston, Massachusetts, called the Latin Quarter. He moved his young family to Brookline, a middle-class

Barbara Walters in 1980, the year she won or shared three Emmy Awards.

suburb of Boston, then to Miami Beach, then to New York City, each time opening a new Latin Quarter club. Barbara at first was embarrassed that her father owned nightclubs, but she came to realize that meeting all the celebrities who frequented the clubs later made her more relaxed in her interviews with the stars.

When she entered the private high school Birth Wathen in New York, Barbara had dreams of becoming an actress, a writer, or a teacher. She explored all three at Sarah Lawrence College in Bronxville, New York, while she earned excellent grades and a bachelor's degree in English. She decided on a career in broadcasting.

In 1951, after Walters graduated from college, she got part-time secretarial jobs until her father helped her get a job writing press releases at WNBC, the New York City NBC television affiliate. Television was still new on the scene but a growing trend in the early 1950s. Female broadcasters, however, were a rarity. Barbara Walters wanted to change this.

She got a break behind the scenes in 1953 when the station hired her as the producer of a live, 15-minute, daily children's show called *Ask the Camera*. When the show was canceled the next year, Barbara landed a job booking guests and generating story ideas for the CBS *Morning Show*. She also married 34-year-old Robert Katz. Barbara Walters's life seemed to be falling perfectly into place.

Barbara excelled at her job, and her responsibilities increased. She conducted some breakthrough interviews with survivors of the crash between the ocean liners *Stockholm* and *Andrea Doria* in 1956. But the *Morning Show* itself was deteriorating, and in 1957, it was canceled. The following year, Barbara and Katz divorced. At about the same time, Barbara's father, Lou Walters, declared bankruptcy.

The Today *show team in the early 1970s: (left to right) Walters, Joe Garagiola, Frank Blair, and Frank McGee.*

Suddenly, it was up to Barbara to support herself. The men in her life were no longer willing or able to support her. Despite her experience, Barbara had trouble finding another job in television and instead wrote press releases for local television and radio producers. While the salary was low, the experience proved invaluable for Walters. She met many of the people who were hiring for television positions, and her writing got better. She eventually landed a job as a staff writer for NBC's *Today* show. Occasionally Walters appeared in front of the camera as a stand-in for the *"Today* girl," actress Pat Fontaine. It was on one of these occasions that Walters got her big break.

On November 22, 1963, President John F. Kennedy was assassinated, and Walters stayed on the air reporting the events for five continuous hours. Everyone at the station was impressed by her professionalism, and less than a year later Walters became the new *Today* girl, partly because the show's anchor, Hugh Downs, campaigned on her behalf.

Most of the former *Today* girls had been beauty queens and actresses. While Walters was attractive, she was not known for her glamour. She had a

Boston accent and a lisp, two unique and undesirable qualities for broadcast journalism. She believed that all these characteristics made her target audience—women—like her more. "I'm a kind of well-informed friend," Walters said. "They don't want me to be glamour[ous] and that's fine. It means I won't have to quit and have face-lifts after forty: I'm in a different category."

Walters's personal life was also in an upswing. In December 1963 she married producer and theater-owner Lee Guber. In 1968, after Barbara had three miscarriages, the couple adopted a baby, whom they named Jacqueline Dena after Walters's sister and mother. "Jacqueline has been the home," Walters later said in a 1985 interview with *McCall's* magazine. "[S]he is what makes it a home. I wanted a child *very, very* badly. You have to want a child very badly if you're in this business. I made the choice. I was not young; I already had a career."

In her first years as a full-fledged reporter, Walters landed interviews with entertainer Fred Astaire, diplomat Henry Kissinger, and former first lady Mamie Eisenhower. Walters herself had become a celebrity. She handled her new status and her assignments as well as any man in her field. But many people criticized Walters for being ruthless, a quality for which many of her male counterparts were praised. Nothing seemed to get in the way of Barbara's getting her story. In the 1960s she handled such controversial subjects as sexual dysfunction, birth control pills, and marijuana use.

In 1970, Walters published a book, *How to Talk with Practically Anybody About Practically Everything*, detailing her own secrets of success. The book discussed business and personal etiquette, including how to write thank-you notes, how to mingle at parties, and how to deal with difficult people. The book became a bestseller and added to Walters's growing popularity. In the early 1970s she made several of the lists of the top women in the country, including *Harper's Bazaar*'s "100 Women of Accomplishment," *Time*'s "200 Leaders of the Future," and the *Ladies' Home Journal*'s "75 Most Important Women."

Walters felt that she was ready for another big career move: a network news anchor position. When she renewed her contract with NBC in 1973, Walters negotiated

In October 1976 Walters debuted on the ABC evening news, coanchoring with Harry Reasoner.

nearly a half million dollars and added a clause that she be named cohost of *Today* when host Frank McGee left the show. A year later, McGee died of bone cancer. And on April 22, 1974, Walters became the first TV news female cohost on network television. In 1975, she won an Emmy Award for her work on the show. But after more than 12 years, Walters was growing weary of her partnership with the network. She wanted more money and independence, and she hoped she could find these somewhere else.

ABC, in last place in the evening news ratings, wanted Walters to coanchor a weeknight newscast. The network offered Walters a nightly newscast, prime-time specials, and an unprecedented $1 million yearly salary. NBC did not want to lose their star, but while they could match the money that ABC was offering, they could not match the prime-time special offer. In 1976, Walters signed a five-year contract with ABC. The record-breaking deal drew criticism from the public. The comedy-skit show *Saturday Night Live* introduced the character "Baba

Wawa," a parody of Barbara Walters with an exaggerated speech impediment.

In October 1976, *ABC News with Harry Reasoner and Barbara Walters* debuted. Reasoner did not believe he should have to share the camera with a woman, and especially did not believe that she should be paid a million dollars. There was tension between Reasoner and Walters from the start, and the pair never clicked. Moreover, Walters was not a news reader but an interviewer. "From the day I was hired, I asked them not to put me on the air *just* to read," Walters admitted. Reasoner resigned in June 1978, and the network moved Walters from the news anchor position to handle celebrity interviews. Walters's second marriage ended in divorce the same year, partly because of the stress Barbara was under at work.

The divorce left Walters unsure about her attempts to juggle career, marriage, and motherhood. Still, in 1980, Walters won two Emmy Awards for Best News Program Segments and Best News and shared a third Emmy for Best News and Documentary Program for her work on *Nightline*. In 1981, Walters interviewed legendary actress Katharine Hepburn, and the two discussed woman's struggle to "have it all." Walters said she considered herself lucky to have been given the opportunities that she has had in life.

The following year, Walters signed a new contract with ABC. She would have three specials of her own, appear regularly on the newsmagazine *20/20*, and stand in sometimes for David Hartman on *Good Morning, America* and for Ted Koppel on *Nightline*.

The 1980s was the decade of the *Barbara Walters Specials*. In 1983 Walters won another Emmy Award for Best Interviewer, and she won two more in 1985 for her specials. She found a more serious forum for her interviews when she joined Hugh

Downs as coanchor of *20/20*. Downs, who had helped Walters get her break some 20 years earlier, proved a good teammate for her.

On May 11, 1986, Walters married for the third time. Her new husband, Merv Adelson, was the chairman of Lorimar Productions. Because of his job, Adelson lived in Los Angeles, while Walters lived in New York. The two had a long-distance marriage for six years before they divorced.

The same year that she married Adelson, Walters landed interviews with Adnan Khashoggi and Manucher Ghorbanifar, two men who played key roles in a notorious arms deal between Iran and the Contras of Nicaragua. But the interview proved disastrous for Walters. Ghorbanifar gave her documents that he asked her to deliver to President Ronald Reagan. She didn't realize that by delivering those papers, she "violated a literal interpretation of news policy," as ABC later admitted. She not only acted as a private messenger for the government, she had withheld the message's content from the public.

While the public may have been angry with Walters, the incident did not affect her salary demands. She renewed her contract for an annual salary of nearly $3 million. She had proved her worth to the ABC network.

In the 1990s, in her sixties, Walters showed no signs of slowing her hectic pace. She continued to get exclusive interviews with top celebrities and newsmakers. In 1994, Walters interviewed the family of Ron Goldman, the young man murdered with the ex-wife of O. J. Simpson. On September 29, 1995, 29 million Americans watched Walters speak with paralyzed actor Christopher Reeve and his wife, Dana. It was Reeve's first interview since he had been thrown from the back of a horse. "I think this

Walters poses with actor Christopher Reeve in September 1995, during the first interview he gave after being paralyzed in an accident.

interview had a greater effect than anything that I have done in all the years at ABC," Walters said afterward.

In 1996, Walters celebrated a special honor, her 20th-anniversary broadcast with ABC. She also received two awards—the prestigious George Foster Peabody Award for her interview with Christopher and Dana Reeve and the first Excellence in Media Award from the Gay and Lesbian Alliance Against Defamation for her interview with HIV-positive Olympic diving gold medalist Greg Louganis.

Walters made a decision in 1997 that surprised even herself. She agreed to return to daytime television as occasional star and executive producer of

The View. In addition to Walters appearing a few times a week to head the show, four other women in different stages of their lives, from widely different backgrounds, cohost the show. Walters joins them on a set that looks like a living room as they interview celebrities and talk about current events and life-style topics.

Barbara Walters today is one of America's most famous news personalities. She won the 1997 Distinguished Service Award from the National Association of Broadcasters, and in 1990 she was inducted into the Academy of Television Arts and Sciences Hall of Fame. In a profession where women have had a difficult time lasting, Walters approaches her seventies with the same resolve she had as she approached her fifties: "When I was young I didn't feel that there was anything that I could do well. . . . In the last few years I've realized that it isn't all luck, that I am good at what I do."

DIANE SAWYER

In 1994, the media played up a dispute between Barbara Walters and fellow broadcast journalist Diane Sawyer. They coanchored similar shows, both on ABC, Sawyer on *Prime-Time Live*, Walters on *20/20*. The media claimed Sawyer and Walters were in fierce competition for the same stories and guests. But the two women maintained that their rivalry was friendly and that they were willing to share the spotlight. In a joint interview with Walters for the magazine *Vanity Fair,* Sawyer suggested that the fact that they were both women lay behind their willingness to play fair. "I can't imagine [that] the same level of disclosure and intimacy and collegiality took place before women got into the business," she said.

Sawyer remembers what it was like before women were permitted in front of the camera reporting the news. For years as a young woman, she had fought for her position and worked hard to become one of the most celebrated broadcast journalists.

She was born Lila Diane Sawyer on December 22, 1945,

Diane Sawyer conducts an interview during the debut of the ABC news program PrimeTime Live.

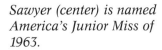

Sawyer (center) is named America's Junior Miss of 1963.

in Glasgow, Kentucky. Her father, E.P., was a lawyer and eventually became a county administrative judge, and her mother, Jean, taught third grade. Diane always looked up to her talented and outgoing sister, Linda, who was three years older than she. The family moved to Louisville, Kentucky, not long after Diane was born.

Besides her schoolwork, in which she excelled, Diane took ballet and tap dancing classes, studied piano, voice, fencing, and the guitar, acted in the theater, and learned how to ride a horse (a favorite pastime in Louisville, which hosts the Kentucky Derby each May). She was determined not to live in the shadow of her sister, who was named runner-up in the state's Junior Miss Pageant and seemed to be good at everything. At Seneca Lake High School, Diane joined many clubs and was editor-in-chief of the school newspaper, *The Arrow*. Seneca's principal, Kenneth B. Farmer, said, "Diane was an honor student from seventh grade on. It would be easier to list the things she didn't accomplish. That list would be far smaller."

At age 17, before she even graduated from high school, Diane became a national celebrity by winning the Junior Miss title for 1963. Diane's poise, speaking ability, quick thinking, and beauty had launched her on a path that would take her to a career in broadcast journalism.

The Junior Miss title required Diane to travel all over the country, giving speeches and attending conventions. But it also brought an $11,000 college scholarship that allowed her to attend Wellesley College in Massachusetts, where Linda was in her junior year.

Despite her beauty and all of her qualifications, Diane often felt insecure at Wellesley. The all-female student body at the prestigious school was highly intellectual and gifted. Despite her fears, Sawyer threw herself into choral group, theatrical productions, and student government with as much gusto as she had displayed in high school. But when she graduated in 1967 with a bachelor's degree in English, Diane had no idea what she wanted to do next.

She knew she loved to write. Add to that her love for performing and working with people, and there was a career in television, her father told her. Back home in Louisville, Sawyer got a job at WLKY-TV, the local ABC station, as weather girl and part-time reporter. Diane now looks back on these years and laughs: "I was a terrible weather girl. I was so bad at it." She had no meteorology background or interest in weather. These drawbacks caused Sawyer to make a lot of errors on the air, only multiplied by her bad eyesight—reading the weather map was difficult without glasses, which of course the glamorous weather girls were not allowed to wear.

But despite her mistakes, at her first job Diane developed the poise and composure in front of the camera for which she is well-known today. Eager to progress, she asked the station manager for more challenging and interesting work. She was soon promoted to full-time news correspondent.

Shortly after her promotion, her father was killed in a car crash while driving to work early one morning. Less than a year after her father's death, Diane left Louisville to look for a job in Washington, D.C. Because of her father's big dreams for her and his support for her career, she felt that he would have been proud of her decision.

"Now I know this may sound incredibly naive," Sawyer says, looking back at her arrival in the nation's capital at age 24. "But when that plane landed at National Airport, I got off with a very firm idea of where I wanted to work. At the White House. True, in the eyes of official Washington I might be right off the equivalent of the turnip truck, but working in the White House was exactly what I had in mind!"

Once again, Diane's father helped her career. His reputation as a Republican judge won her an interview with Ron Ziegler, the White House press secretary to Republican president Richard Nixon. The press secretary's job is to deal with the media, explaining events, making announcements, and handling some public relations for the president. Diane landed a job as assistant to Jerry Warren, the White House deputy press secretary.

From the start, Diane received important assignments at the White House, such as writing press releases and helping draft some of the president's public statements. Within a year, she was promoted to administrative assistant and was then made staff assistant.

Working for President Richard Nixon in the early 1970s, Sawyer remained on the president's staff during the Watergate scandal between 1972 and 1974. She kept track of the events and handled media coverage as the evidence against the president mounted. Nixon and members of his reelection committee were believed to be involved in the break-in and tapping of phones at Democratic National Headquarters at the Watergate Hotel, and an investigation ensued. Hidden funds came to light, along with more illegal spying activities that could be traced back to the president. Meanwhile, President Nixon publicly denied any knowledge of or involvement in the scandal.

As an assistant to White House press secretary Ron Ziegler, Sawyer (left) helps him greet guests on a White House tour in 1972.

But his guilt became clear as the Senate committee investigating the affair listened to taped recordings of the president's private telephone conversations. Some of the tapes were missing and others were erased.

Despite his apparent guilt, Sawyer remained loyal to President Nixon. But he resigned on August 9, 1974, before impeachment proceedings began. He was later pardoned for his part in the Watergate scandal by President Gerald Ford. Even though he left Washington, D.C., Nixon continued to employ some of his aides, including Sawyer.

For the next four years, Sawyer lived in Nixon's hometown of San Clemente, California. She had become an expert on Watergate, and she was in charge of organizing the hundreds of files on the subject. She also helped write Nixon's autobiography, *RN*. The project required that she spend many hours interviewing and working with the former president. It was fascinating, she says, "to watch him reconstruct his life and search through the past to examine the way it defined his destiny, to hear him talk about the people he met, the difference they made. It was taxing, it was exhausting, and it was a graduate education to exceed any other."

When Diane left California to return to Washington, D.C., many of her fellow reporters ignored or avoided her. By supporting and working for Nixon, she had damaged her credibility. But Bill Small, the senior vice president of the CBS News Washington bureau, knew that Sawyer was incredibly smart and talented. He would have hired her 10 years earlier, when she was fresh from Wellesley, but a hiring freeze had stopped him. Now he made Diane a general assignment reporter at CBS. She worked harder and even longer hours to gain back the respect of the people in her profession.

Diane caught the public's attention when, in 1979, she covered the events at Three Mile Island, a nuclear power plant near Harrisburg, Pennsylvania. A cooling system on a nuclear reactor failed, and many people feared there would be a nuclear explosion. Despite the danger involved, Sawyer covered the 12–day crisis on location in Pennsylvania, an impressive figure with a cool demeanor and excellent reporting skills. She was soon promoted to correspondent and then given the sought-after State Department beat in February 1980.

By the time she covered the Iranian hostage crisis, where U.S. hostages were being held by Islamic fundamentalists at the U.S. embassy in Teheran, Iran, Diane had won the nation's admiration and respect. She soon became a regular on the CBS News *Sunday Morning Show.*

In 1981, at age 35, Diane got the biggest break of

In 1981 Sawyer teamed with Charles Kuralt on a CBS morning news show.

her career. CBS network heads asked her to move to New York City to coanchor a new 90-minute morning show they hoped to call *Morning with Charles Kuralt and Diane Sawyer.* Sawyer and Kuralt proved to be a compatible team, and the show's ratings rose. While she was not making as much money as fellow broadcast journalist Barbara Walters, Sawyer still earned an impressive $800,000 a year. *Morning*'s ratings dropped when Charles Kuralt left the show in 1982 and Bill Kurtis was hired as Diane's coanchor. But Sawyer was already being considered for a shot at prime time.

In 1984, Sawyer joined the on-air staff of the previously all-male television show *60 Minutes*. This was broadcast journalism's big time. She was working with the biggest names in her field, including Mike Wallace, Harry Reasoner, Morley Safer, and Ed Bradley.

Her first story for *60 Minutes* nabbed a lot of attention. It was about a North Carolina grandmother set to become the first woman executed in the United States in 22 years. Sawyer had clearly proven herself to be above the typical "women's" stories, which focused on areas such as home or fashion. She also reported on the welfare system and the life of a malnourished young boy in Mali (the boy was consequently adopted by an American couple), and she conducted countless interviews with celebrities and political personalities.

Diane Sawyer's star was on the rise. She was a recognizable face and by 1986 was earning the sizable sum of $1.2 million a year.

While her hectic work days often lasted almost 18 hours, Diane found time for her other interests—including going to movies, cooking, reading, and exercising. She also found time for love in her life with director-producer Mike Nichols. The couple married on April 29, 1988.

"Women are an important economic and cultural force in this country," Diane said in 1986. "I think all women look forward to the day when there's a woman as coanchor of the evening news." Less than three years after that prediction, Sawyer left CBS and *60 Minutes* for a coanchor spot on ABC's *PrimeTime Live*. She joined Sam Donaldson behind the news desk. The partnership eventually clicked.

Today, Diane still works for ABC News, she is still married to Mike Nichols, and—despite their being

Sawyer with her husband, Mike Nichols, at the 1994 premiere of a film he directed.

employed by the same network—she is still seen as competing with *20/20* colleague Barbara Walters. But it is clear that Diane Sawyer has proven that she has the talent to make a name for herself.

ELLEN GOODMAN

A journalist is only as good as her last story, the saying goes, but when Ellen Holtz Goodman won the Pulitzer Prize for commentary in 1980, she proved that she was as good as her last several hundred. Today, her columns run in more than 440 newspapers across the country.

Goodman was born Ellen Holtz on April 11, 1941, in Newton, Massachusetts, a suburb of Boston. Her father was a prominent lawyer who twice ran for a Democratic seat in Congress. Although he was never elected, Jackson Holtz taught Ellen and her older sister, Jane, how to debate, and win, an argument. He emphasized the importance of politics and public issues. Ellen's mother, Edith, was a housewife who supported both of her daughters in their eventual career choices. Both girls became journalists. Ellen's childhood was comfortable and happy. "I wanted to live in the same house, go to the same school, keep the same friends . . . forever."

And so, after she graduated from the Buckingham School, Ellen attended Radcliffe College in nearby Cambridge, Mass-

Ellen Goodman's column is syndicated in hundreds of newspapers across the United States.

achusetts. In college, she performed in musicals, including *Guys and Dolls, On the Town,* and *Damn Yankees.* In June 1963, Goodman graduated with honors, with a degree in modern European history. A few days later, she married her boyfriend, Anthony Goodman, who was a student at Cornell Medical School in Ithaca, New York. And Ellen left home for the first time.

"Prejudice was so overt," Ellen recalls of the workplace she entered as a recent college graduate. Goodman got a job as a researcher in the television department of *Newsweek.* "It took a lot of maturity to be aware of the outrage you felt, and to learn to find a different way to be able to do what you wanted."

In 1965, the Goodmans moved to Michigan, where Anthony completed residency training for his medical degree at the University of Michigan. Ellen decided to try and get a job at the newspaper the *Detroit Free Press.* The managing editor, impressed with her writing ability, offered her a spot as a general assignment reporter. Two years later Anthony's job took them back east to Boston.

Happy to be near her family again, Ellen used her newspaper experience and recommendations from her former employer to land a job as a feature writer at the *Boston Globe*'s women's department. Although she was supposed to write about "soft news"—fashion, cooking, and the home—Goodman couldn't keep her knowledge of political issues out of her writing. Fortunately, the *Globe* opened the editorial page to women writers and their issues in 1970, and Goodman's articles were regularly featured on this prestigious page. In 1974, Ellen's column was titled *At Large.*

In 1968, Anthony and Ellen had a baby daughter, Katherine Anne. Six weeks after Katie was born, Ellen was back at work. While she now appeared

The women's movement of the early 1970s helped inspire Goodman to study the social changes of the time.

to have everything, both a family and a career, her marriage was deteriorating. In 1971, she and Anthony divorced.

Women of Ellen's mother's time usually married, stayed home, and never divorced, but the women of the 1960s and 1970s often felt the pressure of balancing the demands of work and home. Consequently, the divorce rate during this time increased. It was a time of great social change in America. "The women's movement taught a lot of us that the personal is political and the political is personal. You can't deal with those things and make a whole lot of sense out of life—and I think that is crucial to some of what I try to do. To draw the sense out of things," Goodman said.

Goodman decided she wanted to study this social change. In 1974, she drafted a proposal and received a Neiman Fellowship at Harvard. The fellowship granted Goodman money to research and write her first book, *Turning Points.* The book was published in 1979 to critical acclaim. Doris Grumbach in the *New York Times* called it one of the many source books "from one which the full history of these revolutionary times will be written."

While she was writing the book, Goodman's columns were brought to the attention of William B. Dickinson, the general manager and editorial director of the Washington Post Writers Group. He wanted to run the column on the *Post*'s editorial page and possibly syndicate it. As the first woman to write directly for and about women, Goodman attracted a new readership to the *Washington Post.*

"At first the column sold by word of mouth. It was the kind of thing women would clip out and put on the refrigerator," Dickinson said. "Sure it was read by men, but it was taken to heart by women."

"I didn't want to write just light stuff or just politics," Goodman said of her writing. "I felt it was important to do both. I wanted to break through this false dichotomy because people don't live all one way or the other. I didn't want to draw lines between private lives and public lives but rather to connect these lives."

In 1976, *At Large* was syndicated in 25 newspapers. Ten years later, 388 papers ran Goodman's column, and by the mid-1990s the daily column reached more than 440 newspapers nationwide.

In 1980, a year before she turned 40, Ellen Goodman became a household name when she won the Pulitzer Prize for distinguished commentary. It was her article entitled "From a Dropout of the Sixties to a Burnout in the Seventies" that won her the Pulitzer. The story told of a meeting between two people who had been acquaintances in the sixties and found they had little in common in the late seventies. It was both touching and true for many people who lived through this generation. After Goodman won the prize, a string of television interviews and public-speaking appearances followed.

Ellen Goodman has written about topics like parenting, divorce, feminism, alternative life-styles, and current events. Her 750-word columns were so popular that they were compiled into five books: She published *Close to Home* in 1979, *At Large* in 1981,

Keeping in Touch in 1985, *Making Sense* in 1989, and *Value Judgments* in 1993.

Her professional life had never been better when Ellen married her colleague *Boston Globe* national editor Bob Levey in 1982. They moved to the Boston suburb of Brookline and renovated a 19th-century house. Her aunt and uncle live next door, her older sister, Jane Holtz Kay, also lives in the neighborhood, and Ellen's mother lives in nearby Cambridge, Massachusetts. Ellen's father died in 1966. Throughout most of her life, Ellen has managed to stay within a few miles of where she spent her happy childhood.

Since winning the Pulitzer Prize, Goodman was awarded the American Society of Newspaper Editors Distinguished Writing Award in 1980, the Hubert H. Humphrey Civil Rights Award in 1988, the President's Award from the National Women's Political Caucus in 1993, and the American Woman Award by the Women's Research and Education Institute in 1994.

Beginning in January 1996, she spent five months at Stanford University in California as the first Lorry I. Lokey Professor in Professional Journalism. In March 1996, she gave a lecture on personal politics at the university entitled "Politics: Up Close and Too Personal." While she spoke mostly of her experiences, her writing techniques, and media coverage of the presidency and other political figures, she also described a conversation she overheard her daughter and a friend have when they were young children:

"What does your mom do?" asked the friend. "She's a columnist," replied Katie. "What's that?" her friend asked. "Well, my mother gets paid for telling people what she thinks." Today, Goodman continues telling people what she thinks, and her admiring audience continues to grow.

Goodman discussing her landmark book Turning Points. *Despite her wide-ranging commentaries, she has been content to spend most of her life in the region where she grew up.*

HANNAH STORM

As a little girl, Hannah Storm went to basketball games with her dad, Mike Storen, who was general manager of the Kentucky Colonels, a team in the American Basketball Association (ABA). Mike Storen was well known in the world of professional basketball. He would go on to manage the Atlanta Hawks in the National Basketball Association (NBA) and finally would serve as commissioner of the ABA. Because of the nature of her father's business, Hannah got used to traveling and learned all about the game of basketball. Today, Storm is one of the most recognized faces in the world of sports broadcasting—perhaps the only recognizable woman's face in a field of men.

Storm was born Hannah Storen in 1962, in Oak Park, Illinois. Growing up in the 1960s and 1970s when the women's movement was strong, Hannah saw more and more women working outside of the home in jobs that were typically considered "male." It was no longer unusual to be treated by a female doctor, see a female lawyer in the courtroom, or witness women financiers working on Wall Street, a famous

Hannah Storm is probably the best-known woman in the field of sports broadcasting.

street of financial institutions in New York City. Women like Barbara Walters and Diane Sawyer were making a name for women in broadcasting. But there were no women broadcasting sports.

Storm knew before she entered college that she wanted to be a sports broadcaster. "[The sports profession] trickled down to me by osmosis," Storm said. When she thought about careers, she "immediately thought 'sports' [broadcasting], even though no women were doing sports broadcasting, because it felt so natural."

An outstanding high school student, Storm decided to attend the University of Notre Dame in South Bend, Indiana, a school with both a good academic reputation and prestigious sports teams. She went to college in the fall of 1979 and quickly chose two majors: communications and political science. She believed these two fields of study, combined with her growing knowledge of most major sports, would give her a good background for broadcasting.

Notre Dame was also a perfect place for an aspiring sportscaster. Whether the event was a Saturday afternoon football game, an evening basketball game, or an early morning swim meet, Storm was usually there. She also got hands-on experience as a broadcaster at the university's television station, WNDU-TV.

In the spring of 1983, as graduation day approached, Storm went on job interviews. She was surprised by the attitudes of those hiring. "All I heard was the same refrain: 'Oh, I'm not sure if our audience will like it if we put a woman on to do sports.'" Frustrated by this old-fashioned attitude, Hannah took a job as a radio disc jockey at the hard-rock radio station KNCN-FM in Corpus Christi, Texas.

For radio, Hannah Storen called herself Hannah

Storm. "They wanted me to make it Anna Storm," she recalled, "but I said, 'Please leave me something of myself.' " While the radio station was good on-air experience for the recent graduate, Hannah wanted to be in front of the camera. She moved to the larger metropolitan city of Houston and broke into local television there.

At KTXH-TV in Houston, Storm got to try on a variety of broadcasting roles—news reporting, handling studio host assignments, and anchoring the news. An anchor is the person who heads up the news program. Anchors usually comment on reporters' stories and open and close the broadcast.

In March 1988, as Storm's five-year college reunion approached, she was offered a job at WPCQ-TV in Charlotte, North Carolina. There she served as weekend anchor and sports reporter. She was finally doing the kind of reporting that she had dreamed of since she was a little girl!

A year later, Cable News Network (CNN) offered her a better job. The largest cable news network, CNN broadcasts the news 24 hours a day, seven days a week. CNN was a breakthrough in news broadcasting. Before the channel began to broadcast in 1980, the news was broadcast only several times a day on major and local networks.

At CNN, Storm was one of only three women in the 75-member sports department. She was given national exposure at the network. While her career was in an upswing, Hannah met and fell in love with Dan Hicks. Hicks was a fellow sports broadcaster who covered golf, tennis, and football, along with other sports. The two began dating and were soon a couple. It helped that they were both in the same profession—they understood the time and hard work their field demanded. They were married several years later.

Basketball is Storm's first love, and fittingly she became the play-by-play announcer for the first season of the Women's National Basketball Association, teaming up with Lisa Malosky (left) and Ann Meyers.

As the anchor of *CNN Sports Tonight, CNN Sports Saturday,* and *CNN Sports Sunday,* Storm became a recognizable on-air personality. In 1990 she served as cohost for the telecast of the 1990 Goodwill Games, and during the 1992 Winter Olympics she anchored a Sunday night half-hour program, *The Games of '92.* Storm could not have been happier with her career. She had been at CNN for three years and was 30 years old.

But when Storm learned that NBC was interested in hiring both her and Dan, the two packed their bags and moved to Manhattan.

"From the day we were lucky enough to hire her away from CNN, we knew we had something special," NBC sports network head Dick Ebersol said. For her first NBC assignment, Hannah traveled to Wimbledon to cover the All England Tennis Championships. In the summer of 1992, she was paired with Jim Lampley to cohost a 90-minute late-night Olympic show from Barcelona, Spain. She also served as one of the afternoon broadcast's rotating studio hosts for those Olympic Games.

Storm felt a yearning for old times when she was

named one of the cohosts of *Notre Dame Saturday*, a pregame and halftime show on NBC. She remembered sitting in the stands at her old alma mater, Notre Dame, cheering on the team. She continued football commentating at the 1993 Cotton Bowl and the 1994 New Year's Day bowl games. Once she had proved herself as good at reporting the games as any of her male counterparts, Storm was named primary sideline reporter for National Football League (NFL) games on NBC.

Baseball was next. Hannah was a reporter for the 1994 and 1996 Major League All-Star games and pregame host of NBC's coverage of the 1995 World Series.

But basketball has always been Storm's favorite sport. In the late spring of 1996, as she prepared to go to Atlanta for the Summer Olympics, she got a call from NBC sports president Dick Ebersol: Would she host *NBA Showtime* starting in March 1997 while regular host Bob Costas took six months off? Hannah was thrilled. By coincidence, she later told *TV Guide* magazine, she had been about to call NBC to tell them she was going to have a baby.

Despite her pregnancy, Storm kept up her rigorous schedule. She planned to take the *NBA Showtime* position and to cover the Olympics too. Her husband was also traveling to Atlanta for the Olympics to cover the swimming and diving events. Hannah had been researching the Games for over a year. "Even the most cynical viewers can't help but be touched," she said. "These are athletes everybody can relate to. They're not all megastars. They are people who have struggled. Everyday people who have followed their dreams. We have to make people at home understand their struggles."

Her days covering the Olympics were often 15 hours long. On Saturday, July 27, at 1:40 A.M., Storm

Closing a WNBA telecast, Storm (right) and Ann Meyers provide expert analysis.

was tired and rattled when news of an explosion in Centennial Park in Atlanta reached her. She stayed on the air for nearly an hour covering the event. "Absolutely it was the most dramatic thing I've been through on the air," she said.

The most dramatic event of her off-the-air life happened on January 7, 1997, when her daughter, Hannah Elizabeth, was born. Hannah Elizabeth—Hannah Beth, or H.B., as the family calls her—is often with her mom just off camera as Storm is broadcasting.

Besides hosting *NBA Showtime*, in the summer of 1997, Storm called the play-by-play action of the very first season of the Women's National Basketball Association (WNBA). "Not only is this league an opportunity for women to play professionally where none existed before, it opens up an entire new avenue for me," Storm said.

Hannah Storm has proven that she can deal with any situation, on or off camera. In 1995, baseball player Albert Belle assaulted her verbally during Game 3 of the World Series. Belle later said he had thought that she was a different reporter. Storm was again the object of anger when NBA star Charles Barkley blamed her and NBC for misinterpreting comments he made about his team—the Houston Rockets—during an interview. Both Belle and Barkley later apologized to Storm.

In 1997, Storm's talent and dedication to her field earned her an Emmy Award nomination for outstanding sports personality/studio host. The other nominees, including Bryant Gumbel and Jim Nantz, were all male.

Not only is Hannah Storm making a name for herself in sports broadcasting, she is making sure that women have the chance to call plays on the air. She has joined the long and prestigious list of women who have become pioneers in broadcasting and journalism.

CHRONOLOGY

1700s In Colonial America, 16 of 78 newspapers are edited by women.

1849 Amelia Bloomer starts *Lily,* the first woman-run paper for women, put out by female typesetters.

1853 Mary Ann Shadd becomes the first African-American editor, cofounding the *Provincial Freeman* in Canada.

1882 The Woman's National Press Association forms, with Emily Edson Briggs as president.

1904 Muckraking journalist Ida Tarbell publishes *The History of Standard Oil,* which leads to a federal investigation of the company.

1914 Edna Woolman Chase becomes editor-in-chief of the fashion magazine *Vogue.*

1915 Mary Roberts Rinehart becomes the first female foreign war correspondent when she goes to Europe to cover World War I for the *Saturday Evening Post* magazine.

1929 Bess Furman becomes the first reporter to cover Congress for the Associated Press.

1936 Anne O'Hare McCormick becomes the first woman on the editorial board of the *New York Times.*

1955 Carol Brown becomes the first woman to win a Pulitzer Prize.

1964 Marlene Sanders becomes the first woman to anchor an evening news broadcast when she substitutes on ABC-TV.

1965 Joan Murray becomes the first African-American female journalist hired by a major television news station, CBS.

1974 Helen Thomas becomes the first female to head the White House bureau of the news service United Press International.

1976 Barbara Walters receives an unprecedented $1 million a year and becomes the first woman to coanchor a major network's evening news at ABC.

1980–85 Seven women win Pulitzer Prizes for writing, including Ellen Holtz Goodman for her commentary at the *Boston Globe.*

1983 News anchor Christine Craft sues her station for sexual discrimination after she is fired, she believes, on the basis of her looks.

1995 Hannah Storm becomes the first female to host a weekly network pregame show for a major sport.

FURTHER READING

Belford, Barbara. *Brilliant Bylines: A Biographical Anthology of Notable Newspaperwomen in America*. New York: Columbia University Press, 1986.

Bernikow, Louise. *The American Women's Almanac*. New York: Berkley, 1997.

Blue, Rose, and Joanne E. Bernstein. *Diane Sawyer: Super Newswoman*. Hillside, N.J.: Enslow, 1990.

Heinemann, Sue. *Timelines of American Women's History*. New York: Berkley, 1996.

Hosley, David H., and Gayle K. Yamada. *Hard News: Women in Broadcast Journalism*. New York: Greenwood, 1987.

Mills, Kay. *A Place in the News*. New York: Dodd, Mead, 1988.

Remstein, Henna. *Barbara Walters*. Philadelphia: Chelsea House, 1998.

Thomas, Helen. *Dateline: White House*. New York: Macmillan, 1975.

PHOTO CREDITS

Corbis-Bettmann: pp. 10, 13, 15, 16, 20, 23, 24, 26, 28, 33, 45, 47, 51, 53; AP/Wide World Photos: pp. 18, 31, 38, 40, 43; AP/Wide World Photos/Monika Graff: p. 2; AP/Wide World Photos/Ken Reegan /ABC News: p. 36; Kim Arrington/Washington Post: p. 48; Courtesy NBC/NBA Photos: p. 54; Courtesy NBC Sports: pp. 58, 60.

INDEX

ABOUT THE AUTHOR

Anne E. Hill holds a B.A. in English from Franklin and Marshall College, where she was a member of Phi Beta Kappa and wrote for the *Franklin and Marshall Magazine.* She has also written the Chelsea House titles *Denzel Washington* and *Ekaterina Gordeeva.* She lives in Wayne, Pennsylvania, with her husband, George.